Ba

STOLEN BASES

A trip into the wilderness can get pretty wild!
See why in
TERROR TRAIL

Here's a job that will really haunt you.
Check out
GRAVE DISCOVERY

It's time to face the music! Take a look at
SEE NO EVIL

Who's *really* behind the wall?
See for yourself in
A BONE TO PICK

Who's calling? Get the answer, read
PLEASE CALL BACK!

Somebody's inside . . . but nobody should be.
See who in
ANYBODY HOME?

Someone's planning an *un*welcome.
Find out more in
HOME, CREEPY, HOME

Shop . . . until you drop!
Read all about it in
BUYING TROUBLE

ISBN 0-8114-9301-6
Copyright ©1995 Steck-Vaughn Company. All rights reserved. No part of the material protected by this copyright may be reproduced or utilized in any form or by any means, electronic or mechanical, including photocopying, recording, or by any information storage and retrieval system, without permission in writing from the copyright owner. Requests for permission to make copies of any part of the work should be mailed to: Copyright Permissions, Steck-Vaughn Company, P.O. Box 26015, Austin, TX 78755. Printed in the United States of America.

2 3 4 5 6 7 8 9 9 98 97

Produced by Mega-Books of New York, Inc.
Design and Art Direction by Michaelis/Carpelis Design Assoc.

Cover illustration: Matthew Archambault

MODEM MENACE

by Judy Katschke

interior illustrations by
Marcy Ramsey

CHAPTER 1

Kevin DaCosta sat in the principal's office. He tried to keep his fingers from drumming on the chair arm.

"Kevin DaCosta!" Principal Davis's voice made him jump. "Did you hear what I just said?" she asked.

Kevin nodded. He had heard her all right. He had heard her say he was failing English, big time!

Principal Davis picked up one of Kevin's test papers.

"Kevin, Shakespeare did not write *Hamlet* on a PC," she sighed.

Kevin held back a laugh. He began to explain. "You see . . ."

"What I see is that you could not

think of the right answer. You were desperate to come up with just any answer!" said Principal Davis.

Kevin stared down at his hands and shrugged. He heard the whine of a pencil sharpener behind him. Kevin turned around. There was Ignatius "Iggy" Carbone, dumb grin and all. Iggy had skipped most of his classes last year. Now he was serving time as Principal Davis's office aide.

Principal Davis stood up. "I'm going to make a copy of your grades for your mother," she said. "I'll be right back."

"Gee, thanks," thought Kevin glumly.

Iggy had finished with the pencils. Now he was drowning the plants with water. Kevin ignored him. Instead he studied the corny stuff on Principal Davis's desk. There was a plastic pig in a snow shaker from Kansas City. There was also a goofy pig wearing a cap and gown. A pig stapler held down a sheet of paper with computer codes.

Kevin leaned closer. "Are these the codes and password for all the school files?" he wondered. "Whoa!" thought Kevin. "Getting into those codes would be awesome!" He grabbed the code sheet and stuffed it into his notebook.

"Kevin," sighed Principal Davis as she returned to her desk. "I know you're a bright young man. You just have to study, study, study, and then study some more!"

"I will, I will, I will," replied Kevin. He collected his grades and backed out the door. He bumped right into Iggy Carbone, almost knocking the watering can out of Iggy's hands.

"Watch it!" growled Iggy. Kevin ignored him as he hurried out of the office.

Two hours later, Kevin stood in the

lunch line, his mind still on the code sheet he had taken.

"What will you have, meat loaf or stuffed shells?" asked Flo from behind the cash register.

Kevin had no appetite. "Just a tuna sandwich today," he answered.

Flo slowly pressed the numbers on the rusty old cash register. "Piece of junk," she grumbled.

"Why don't you ask the school to buy you a computerized cash register?" asked Kevin. "It would really speed up the lunch line."

Flo shook her head. "Isn't there anything on your mind besides computers, Kevin?" she asked.

Kevin smiled. Sure there was—Amanda Scott. And she was sitting just a few tables away.

Kevin first met Amanda Scott last year in the Freshman Computer Club. They quickly became good friends. They even had their own secret computer

code names. His was Jimmy B. for the secret agent James Bond. Hers was Amelia E. for the famous pilot Amelia Earhart.

This year Amanda was spending a lot of time with Brian Garner, a stuck-up senior with a flashy car.

Kevin hoped next year would be different. Brian would be out of the way in some college upstate. "And Amanda Scott and I will be juniors," thought Kevin. "That is, if I can pass English."

Chapter 2

"Kevin, what are you doing in there?" Mrs. DaCosta called through the door. "It's after midnight."

"Working on my computer, Ma!" Kevin called back. He switched on his PC.

HEY, DUDE, WHAT'S HAPPENING? flashed onto the screen. Kevin grinned. He was proud of the way he had programmed his computer, "the Duke!"

"As soon as I hook you up to the modem and the telephone, we're set," answered Kevin. The modem was the coolest part of his PC. Together with a telephone and a cable, it helped Kevin go on-line all around the world.

When the hookup was complete, Kevin hit the proper command. LET'S GET STARTED, SHALL WE? responded the Duke.

Kevin typed a phone number on the keyboard. He waited as the modem dialed the number. The sudden sound of three loud beeps made him jump.

TYPE IN PASSWORD appeared on the screen. Kevin checked the school's code sheet. The password was HOG. Kevin remembered the pigs on Principal Davis's desk. "It figures," he thought.

Kevin typed the password HOG and pressed the ENTER key. The screen flickered. Then NORTH HIGH SCHOOL FILES/STARTUP appeared.

"Yes!" Kevin punched the air with his fist. He entered the code for the sophomore class.

"Come on, come on," he whispered. Suddenly he was staring at the class grades!

"Wow!" gasped Kevin. "Peter Lee is acing biology! Amanda Scott is getting straight A's! . . . And Kevin DaCosta is failing English."

Kevin reached for the keyboard. "*Was* failing English," he said, changing the F to a C-.

"All right!" Kevin flashed a wicked grin. "I am on a major roll here!" He decided to check out the rest of the school files.

"The Albert Einstein Scholarship Fund should be interesting," thought Kevin. So he entered the code for "Big Al."

"Two hundred thousand bucks," whistled Kevin. "Big Al, you are looking good!" Then something weird happened. The numbers began to change!

"Hey! I didn't do anything," Kevin cried. $150,000 . . . $140,000 . . . $130,000. The scholarship money was fading fast!

"It's one o'clock in the morning!" thought Kevin. He saw the name BROOKVILLE SAVINGS BANK at the top of the screen. That bank always closes at 3:30 p.m.!

"Wow! Wait'll the cops hear about this!" Suddenly Kevin remembered his own little crime. He gulped.

Kevin's hand paused on the keyboard. HEY, DUDE? WHAT'S HAPPENING? blinked the Duke after a few seconds.

"Don't ask," Kevin groaned quietly. "Just don't ask."

The next day Kevin shuffled through the lunch line in a daze.

"Hey, Kevin," called Flo. "Your wish came true!" She pointed to the brand new computerized cash register on the counter. Kevin's head snapped up. Could Flo have stolen the money for the cash register? Could Flo be the leader of a lunchroom racket?

Kevin sat down at an empty table. He watched Stacey Linden stroll by. She

was sporting a cool new leather jacket.

"Hmmm. You can't buy that with baby-sitting money," thought Kevin. Hey, he had to stop this! He was seeing thieves everywhere he looked!

Kevin tried to study Shakespeare instead. "To go to the police or not to go to the police," he wondered. "That is the question!" Unless, of course, he played detective himself.

CHAPTER 3

"Kevin, are you talking to that computer again?" Mrs. DaCosta called through the door.

"I'm almost done, Ma!" Kevin called back to her.

It was 12:45 a.m. Kevin hooked up his PC to the modem the same way he had the night before. All he had to do now was sit and wait.

"I don't get it, Duke," Kevin told his PC. "In movies and books, spies never have to wait for anything." He yawned. "And they're never sleepy!"

By 1:30 a.m. Kevin's eyes felt like sandbags. "What if there was no thief? What if there was a good reason for the

disappearing money?" he thought.

The screen flickered. Kevin read the words MAKE SELECTION NOW. Then the words TRANSFER FUNDS flashed and disappeared. Big Al's numbers began to change again: $130,000 . . . $120,000 . . . $110,000!

"Hey, knock it off!" Kevin shouted. He shook his computer. The modem began beeping like crazy.

"Now what's going on?" Kevin

demanded. Big Al's numbers disappeared. In their place was a message!

MISSION POSSIBLE, the message read. And it was signed Amelia E.

Kevin blinked. Amelia E.? Amanda? Amanda Scott was the computer thief?

"No way!" shouted Kevin. "There's got to be some mistake!" He reached over and hit a command.

BUMMER, MAN! the Duke flashed. Bummer was right!

Kevin walked to school the next morning wishing his life would be normal again.

"I'll even settle for boring," Kevin muttered. He was so tired he tripped over some kids sitting on the school steps.

"Sorry," mumbled Kevin.

"No problem," came a girl's voice. It was Amanda! She joined him going up the steps.

"I hear you're in hot water," she said.

Kevin spun around. "What do you mean?" he demanded.

"You're failing English, right?" Amanda asked him.

"Oh, yeah," he mumbled. "I guess so."

"Well, at least you're still the champ computer wiz!" As Amanda laughed, Kevin noticed a flashy gold chain around her neck.

"Computers are something you seem

to be a wiz at too, Amelia E.!" he sneered.

Amanda stared at him. "Kevin, are you okay?" she asked.

Kevin sat down on the steps. "Amanda, I know all about it, okay?"

He told Amanda about the scholarship money, the message, and Amelia E.

"Kevin, it wasn't me!" cried Amanda.

"Oh, sure," laughed Kevin. "After all, there must be millions of thugs with pictures of Amelia Earhart hanging in their cells!"

"Kevin, I swear to you, it wasn't me!" Amanda insisted.

Kevin looked into Amanda's eyes. Somehow he knew she was telling the truth. "Then who would use your code name?" he asked her.

"The only other person who knows about Amelia E. is Brian," said Amanda. "But Brian would never do such a horrible thing!"

At that moment, Brian Garner drove up in his car.

"Hey, Amanda," he called. "Come check out my new CD player!"

"Yeah, right," muttered Kevin.

"Maybe we should call the police," suggested Amanda.

"No! We can't go to the police!" Kevin blurted out. Amanda stared at him. "I mean, I've been doing my own detective work."

"Oh," said Amanda. "May I help?"

"I guess so, if you want to," answered Kevin. "Come over at ten o'clock tonight. And bring some chips," he added.

"Sure! If you make some dip!" called Amanda on her way down the steps to the car.

Kevin watched sadly as Amanda kissed Brian. Then he saw a kid in the back seat of the car making dumb faces. Kevin looked closer. It was Iggy Carbone!

CHAPTER 4

"I can't believe you have the password and codes for all of the school files!" exclaimed Amanda. "Show me some more."

"Shhhh!" warned Kevin. "My mom thinks we're working on our homework."

Kevin hit a command on the computer. LET'S GET STARTED, SHALL WE? flashed the Duke.

Kevin typed in the code for the scholarship fund. When Big Al appeared, Amanda Scott studied the screen. "I wonder why the thieves didn't take the money all at once?" she asked.

"It's the old salami trick," said Kevin.

"They thought nobody would notice if the money was taken out slice by slice."

"Got any ideas about what we should do?" asked Amanda.

"I thought I'd reprogram the system to transfer the stolen money back to Big Al," explained Kevin.

Amanda took the keyboard. "First we have to find out where the money went!" she said. After fifteen minutes of keyboard action, Amanda found it. "Ah-ha! The stolen money is at the PATRIOT SAVINGS BANK!"

"In whose account?" asked Kevin.

"Chill out," replied Amanda. "I'm working on it!" She typed LOCATE ACCOUNT on the keyboard. A number appeared, and then a name. Kevin squinted. "Clarence Barker III? What kind of weird name is that?" he wondered out loud.

Amanda fell back in her chair, biting her lip. "It's Brian's dog," she said.

"What are you talking about?" asked

Kevin, confused.

"Brian once had a German Shepherd named Clarence Barker III," said Amanda. "It died a few years ago. Got hit by a . . ."

"That's it!" cried Kevin. "Brian used his dead dog's name to open a phony account! The thief is Brian Garner!"

Amanda was stunned. "No, Brian's

great," she insisted. "See? He gave me this gold chain!"

"Where do you think he got the money for that chain?" Kevin demanded. "But what I want to know is how he got his hands on the school code sheet."

"I bet it was Iggy Carbone," replied Amanda. "He's always in the principal's office. And I don't think he just sharpens pencils and waters plants!"

Kevin could see how upset Amanda was. "Look, you don't have to do this," he said.

"Oh, yes I do!" she exclaimed. "Let's get the creep!"

"Okay!" said Kevin. "First we have to get into Brian's PC. We've got to stop him from stealing even more money."

"I think I can guess his password," Amanda said grimly. She typed in VALENTINE. "Valentine's Day is when we went on our first date," she explained.

"Oh, how romantic!" sneered Kevin. He took back the keyboard and typed in a bunch of codes.

"I think Brian Garner is in for a major surprise," Kevin said as he grinned.

"Perfect," Amanda agreed. Then she grabbed the keyboard from Kevin. "Now for one last touch!" Amanda clicked on a few codes. Suddenly the screen began to blink. Brian was typing commands into his PC!

"If this doesn't work, I'll freak out," said Amanda.

Not moving, Kevin and Amanda watched as a small window popped up on the screen. A message flashed inside the window. FILE LOCKED/COMMAND CANNOT BE EXECUTED!

"Yes!" shrieked Kevin. "It worked!" He punched the air with his fist.

After a few seconds an angry word blazed across the screen: THIEF!!!!!

"All right!" they shouted, slapping high-fives. Amanda reached across the desk for the phone.

"Don't tell me you're calling Brian!" Kevin cried out.

"No. I'm going to call the police!" said Amanda.

"Amanda," Kevin sighed, taking the receiver from her hand. "Before we do that, there's something I've got to tell

you." Kevin's spy days were about to end. The time had come to confess.

A few weeks later, Kevin "Jimmy B." DaCosta sat trapped in his bedroom after school, waiting. He had to spend all his free time tutoring little kids in computers. "This is part of your community service sentence," the judge had explained in court.

Brian Garner had been dumb enough to leave his computer on when he answered the door that fateful night. The police then knew they had the right address. Brian's trial was coming up in the fall. There wouldn't be any college upstate for him this year.

And Iggy? Iggy was *really* sharpening pencils now. He needed them to write to his lawyer!

Kevin felt bad for Amanda. She got detention for the wrongful use of the school computer files. Kevin felt even worse because he hadn't seen her in weeks.

"I guess she doesn't want to be seen with another loser," thought Kevin.

"Kevin!" his mother called from downstairs. "Your next student is on her way up."

Kevin groaned. "If I see one more nine-year-old, I think I will . . ." The door opened. Amanda walked in.

"You must be my tutor," she teased.

Kevin laughed. "What could I possibly teach you about computers?" he asked.

Amanda Scott sat down next to Kevin. "Well, you never did show me how to play Space Attack," she began.

Kevin felt like someone had drop-kicked his heart. "I will, if . . . if you'll help me with my English," he stammered.

"It's a deal," Amanda replied. She shook Kevin's hand and smiled. "Now let's get started, shall we?"